Words from Cats

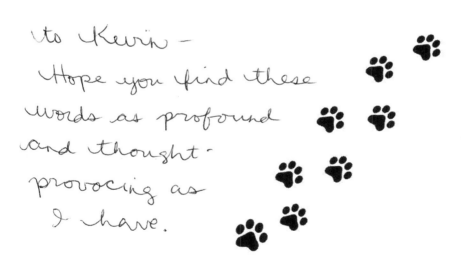

to Kevin –
Hope you find these
words as profound
and thought-
provoking as
I have.

love from yer
        Mom – and all of our kitties!

– November 2019 –

Vanessa Lourenço

Words from Cats

The inspiring words of wisdom your cat wants you
to keep in mind.

Title: Words from Cats

Author: Vanessa Lourenço

English edition: Vanessa Lourenço

Cover: Raquel Vicente

Publisher: Vanessa Lourenço

Vanessa.lourenco@gmail.com

ISBN: 978 - 1986535496

Published in the United States of America

We've all walked the Earth once.

Most of us, many more times

than we can recall.

- Vanessa Lourenço

Acknowledgements

The present book is an assembling of inspiring messages brought to us by the cats in our lives. Thank you Méfis, my angel cat, for the light you brought into my life; thank you Felix, my spiritual animal, for your guidance; thank you Pantufa, my Goddess cat, for your unconditional love. I would also like to thank my mother Alice Lourenço and Visanee Stamtee, my dear friend, for reviewing my work and last but not least, a word of appreciation to each and every cat in the world for honoring your mission of turning us into better human beings, sometimes being completely misunderstood along the way. I see you, and I love you.

Vanessa Lourenço

Prologue

Cats are one of the most popular kind of pets in the world, known to be tiny panthers we can cherish and share our homes with. Usually more independent than dogs, they show us that love also means respecting individuality; they make it clear that sharing life with others doesn't mean you can't enjoy it as an individual as well. You see… they are *our* cats now, but they don't forget they were once wild panthers.

Throughout history and along the past few thousand years, cats have also been considered mystic animals, worshiped by Egyptians and connected to black magic in the middle ages. Even today, no one can deny they're still considered mystical creatures by people all over the world.

Now… what do you think it would happen if you were able to get advice from your own cat? What would he tell you? If you were somehow able to listen to what he has to say, would it make a difference in your life? Would you decide to listen and give some thought to it? Or would you ignore it, thinking "he's just a cat"?

This is what this book is all about. Ever since my early years I've felt drawn to the animal kingdom and since I can ever remember, they have been my reliable guides when it comes to my own personal growth.

I believe there's a sacred place deep inside each one of us in which we can reach out to every living being's soul in this planet and to help enlighten each other's paths…and that includes our feline friends.

I believe anyone can reach this sacred place within. All you need to do is believe that you can and be willing to listen. I hope this book can help you find the way or if you already did, I hope it brings a smile upon your face and a sparkle into your eyes, knowing it is indeed true: our pets never come into our lives by chance, and if we allow them to, they really change our lives forever.

I hope you enjoy reading this book at least as much as I enjoyed writing it. Thank you for showing up.

Vanessa Lourenço

How to read this book

Actually, feel free to read it as you wish.

Nevertheless, there's a specific way I would like you to consider: every time you feel like it or find yourself bewildered, frustrated, angry or just sad, or even if you feel the need to ask the universe for a sign of any kind regarding your life path… close your eyes. Take a few deep breaths, reach for the nearest cat (please be careful if you're not friends with him/her) and look him in the eyes, taking another few deep breaths. If it is your cat, you can even cuddle him for a few seconds. And now you're ready. Reach for this book and close your eyes. Now open it randomly and read what it says.

Did it help?

Vanessa Lourenço

He's a cat, like the rest of us. There are others but this is our story, our path, our pawprints on Earth and beyond it. It's our nature, our soul, our higher purpose. And it's also the story of a cat. Have you ever caught yourself wondering what do cats think when they get their eyes halfway closed and seem to be seeing something we can't? Or when they purr for no reason at all? Your beloved cat can be him and if it is so, he knows. He knows he chose to visit you way before he came down to Earth. He knows just how special you are. The next time you cross paths with one of us, in or out of your house, make no mistake: we know who you are.

Vanessa Lourenço, The black cub of Felis Mal'ak

1. Impossible

He rolled over and stretched up his paws, as if he was trying to reach for the sky. I asked him: "Aren't you a bit too small to challenge the clouds with your claws?"

His paws remained stretched and he stared at me for a second, as if he had no clue about what I was trying to say. And yet, he replied: "Aren't you a bit too big to believe there is such thing as an impossible task?"

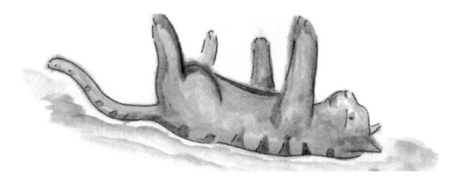

2. Jump

Every now and then he would run around the house as if chasing an invisible villain, jumping everywhere as if his life depended on it. One day I told him: "You shouldn't jump like that, you might hurt yourself."

He came closer for a second, smiling as if he knew a very important secret. He answered: "Always keep in mind, life saves the greatest jumps for those who aren't afraid to fall."

3. Fear

He came to me for no apparent reason, probably guessing I was feeling troubled somehow. He leaned over my leg, looked at me straight in the eyes and stood in silent. A few seconds later I asked: "How do you do it?"

He frowned, looking confused, so I added: "You're always so self-assured, so willing to conquer the world... how do you do it?"

He widened his eyes and smiled, before saying: "First of all, I know you have my back. Besides..."

He went silent, so I asked: "Besides what?"

He smiled again, and I spotted a sparkle in his eyes. He added: "What would you do, if the world didn't scare you so much?"

4. Past

He was a happy cat with a heavy past. Used to seeing him smile, one day I asked him: "Is there anything about your past that you truly miss?"

He stared at me, his eyes full of an overflowing gratitude. And said: "You want to know if I look back and miss something? Yes, not all of it was bad. But I've learned we can miss both friends and places without wishing them to be part of our lives."

5. Immortal

He was a big, black cat. Despite living in the streets, his fur was bright as if nature had decided to reward him for his confidence, the boldness running through his veins and the passionate way the path unfolded under his paws.

Sometimes, he would be absent for weeks and each time I asked myself if I would get to see him again. But he always came back. And every time I got to see him, he presented me with a brighter sparkle in his eyes, the kind of sparkle that is able to make me believe every dream can come true. He didn't survive because he was tough, he survived because he merged into everything that surrounded him. He was one with the world, and the world watched itself through him. It survived in him. The last time we met, he was leaving once more. Serene, confident... free. I've never seen him again, but he was the world. And for that, I'm sure he became immortal.

6. Potential

"Your only true obligation is to stay true to yourself", he told me one day while chasing a fly, "for times will come when you won't be able to meet your higher potential. And that will have to be enough."

7. Selfish

"There's something I don't understand about humans," she told me one day while licking vigorously her paw and rubbing it on her muzzle, "cats are known to be selfish because they act as they please but, for me, being selfish means setting the rules on someone else's life."

8. Jump

He was about to jump, each muscle perfectly drawn under his silky fur. He noticed me right before he did, and I'm sure he read in my face I couldn't believe he was about to jump that far. So he smiled, and said: "The outcome of your boldest jump relies the most on your starting point, and not so much on where you're headed. Not so much on where you'll land, but on why you decided to take the leap in the first place."

9. Like

He was beautiful and fully aware of it. So, one day I said: "You know, not everybody likes cats…"

He licked his paw with his rough tongue and rubbed it on his muzzle, glancing at me as if I were crazy. He answered: "Do you honestly believe we should hope for everyone to like us? To like me isn't anyone else's job… it's mine!"

10. Words

Sitting on the couch, the big gray cat seemed absent. After a while I asked him: "Wouldn't you enjoy being actually able to talk?"

He blinked, almost as if he were waking up from a dream, and stretched out his body. Then he looked me in the eye and said: "You do understand me without using words, don't you?"

I smiled, it was true. But I added: "Just because I understand you, that doesn't mean you are able to talk."

He smiled back, narrowing his eyes and said: "Who needs words, when our attitudes speak so much louder and tell us so much more of who we are and what we long for?"

11. Thirst

He showed up as usual, unnoticed. Always confident, always majestic. He looked me straight in the eye and I could feel both of his deep blue lagoons of wisdom touching my soul. He said: "Cuddle me, and I'll tell you a story."

He usually didn't ask for it, so I got curious. He jumped over my lap and I rubbed him between the eyes. He closed them and said: "Once upon a time there was this stray cat feeling thirsty. He had a clue where to find water but wasn't so sure he would be able to get there."

He interrupted himself for a second and lifted his chin to get rubbed. Then he continued: "On its way towards the water spring, he noticed the surrounding vegetation was all dry and yet he kept going. A little further ahead, he came across several other animals heading back and looking thirsty as well, and one of them told him the vegetation was all dry, so he wouldn't find any water in that direction. He nodded but kept on moving forward and a few minutes later, he found the water spring and drank as much as he needed from the crystal waters."

I frowned, feeling confused. But then he smiled, narrowing his eyes, and added: "You know… life will always test you. But the ones refusing to give up are the hardest ones to beat."

12. Bonkers

He was crazy. Really bonkers. He would chase invisible enemies around the house, attack rugs and ambush innocent paper balls and all kinds of Christmas ornaments. His eyes glowed like a madman and for that, I respected him. It requires both madness and wisdom to look life straight in the eye and demand happiness.

13. Stagnant

"It all comes down to how deeply committed to your dreams you really are", she said to me one day while resting along a shade on a hot day. I was feeling exhausted and pretty much stagnant at the time and had decided to reach for the tabby cat, as she always found a way to make me feel better. And she did by adding: "When your life exhausts you, all you need to do is become aware of the difference between taking a break and giving up."

14. Purr

He was lying next to me, purring, and I finally decided to question him openly about it: "Why do cats purr?"

He stretched out, adjusting his head over the blankets, and slightly opened his eyes before saying: "If I look you deep in the eye, you'll know I love you. But not everyone is ready to find love in the eyes of an animal, so we adopted the purr. That way our love can be heard."

15. Brave

He belonged to a cat colony but unlike the others, he didn't come near to people. One day I asked him from a distance: "Why aren't you as brave as the other cats?"

He shook his head in disappointment and told me: "I was born out here and I've seen many things. Being brave doesn't mean taking unnecessary risks. It means watching what everyone else is doing and still feel free to choose a different path if it feels right to do it."

16. Elder

He was an old, gray cat, every inch of his thin and yet brawny body speaking of many years spent surviving in the streets. One day, I noticed all the other cats avoided him, except one: there was this young black cat coming to meet him every single day. He would rub his dark head on the old cat's chin and every time he did, the elder smiled.

I once approached the black cat and asked him: "Why do you come to him when all the other cats don't?"

The little dark cub stretched his tiny body and looked me in the eye, smiling. He said: "We spend our lives in the streets, where each cat competes with all the others for survival. The Elder… the Elder knows life. He speaks to it. And in exchange, life teaches him the best ways to survive. That makes him a threat to other cats, which are competing for the same life resources. So, they choose to turn their backs on him."

Sadly, that made sense to me, but it wasn't answering my question: "And what about you? Why aren't you following their lead?"

He smiled again, his eyes were sparkling from anticipation. He answered: "Because I don't know how to talk to life yet. And there's no better teacher than the Elder."

17. Luck

He was a stray cat and an impressive hunter as well. Many times before I had seen him pass by me with his prey hanging from his mouth, looking really pleased with himself. His long, silky white coat only added to the huge cat's nobility. One day I told him: "You're really lucky!"

He stopped and blinked before glancing at me and said: "Yes, you can say I'm lucky. But I only began being lucky when I showed life I was willing to fight for my achievements."

18. Cat spirit

Lying down on the green field, it felt as if the entire world experienced itself through him and every mystery had been surfaced through the one he was meant to be. As if every and each one of heaven's stars took rest within his tiny, sparkling eyes during the day, patiently waiting for the night to come to lighten up the sky. He was one among them all, and all of them were made of him. He carried inside him everything worth fighting for.

19. Wild

He carried the sparkle of wild things inside his eyes. The kind of sparkle able to turn the darkness of the night into the dawn that crushes the impossible tasks of the world, and spreads all over the colors of the rainbow. He couldn't be beaten because he refused to give up, he was way more determined than life itself. To witness the world through others' eyes, it seemed to him crueler that death and as any other cat, he faced life with his chin up and his chest wide open. And life presented him all its mysteries in return.

20. Noir

Everyone called him Noir, and he was always surrounded by other cats asking him things such as "where's the cleanest water?" or "which plants can we eat?". And he answered each question with a loving smile, as the streets had no secrets to him. One day, it was my turn to ask: "Don't you ever get tired of teaching them?"

He frowned and glanced at me, his long black tail waving: "Do you know why I survived this far? Because I was never afraid of asking questions. And because I did, I always found the answers. That is the most important lesson I can teach them."

21. Walls

I spotted him standing next to a high wall, seemingly trying to figure out if climbing was within his reach. However, he wasn't even trying, he was just sitting there. As soon as he realized he wasn't alone, he took a deep breath and said: "What can you hear, coming from the other side?"

I listened closer and realized there was a busy road on the other side of the wall. So, he got up and stretched up, before adding: "Sometimes walls in our lives are hidden blessings, protecting us from taking dangerous steps."

22. Seashore

Everyone had already noticed how badly the black cat wanted to get into the sea. Day after day he would get closer to the seashore, yet without ever touching the water with as much as a toe. One day I asked him: "If you're afraid of the water, why do you keep coming back every day?"

He glanced at me, his yellow eyes as fearful as fascinated, and said: "Being afraid does not always mean you're giving up."

23. Vacuum cleaners

He hated vacuum cleaners and yet that day, he was lying on his back under one. So, I had to ask: "Didn't you use to hate vacuum cleaners?"

For a few seconds I thought he couldn't hear me through all that noise. But finally he said, while the vacuum cleaner went back and forward over his belly: "If you ever allow your fears to paralyze you, you'll never overcome them. And life will bring back to you the same obstacles, again and again, until you decide to face them."

24. Fire

The fire was spreading fast through the vegetation near the stream. While trying to stop it, we spotted this huge brown cat entering the water and getting all wet just to run back towards the fire and shake his body near the flames. He did this again and again, so I finally yelled at him: "What are you doing? Stay in the water! Do you want to get burned to death?"

He took a glance at me and said, after entering the water once more: "This is also my home, and I'm only doing my share on trying to save it."

25. Eyes

As many times before, the long-haired cat looked at me straight in the eye, leaving me speechless. It felt as if my entire soul took refuge within his almond eyes, as if somehow inside them, I was able to find the true colors of who I was. Diving into them, I asked him: "Who are you?"

He smiled: "I'm everything my limits didn't stop me from achieving, I'm everything of the obstacles in my life, that it couldn't steal from me. Same as you."

26. Kindness

He would rub his tiny body all over the legs of each person he came across, and I couldn't figure out why. Sometimes he got cuddled, sometimes just ignored and a few other times he was pushed away. And yet he didn't seem to mind, so I asked him: "Why do you keep doing that? One day you may end up getting hurt!"

He stared at me, looking surprised: "Have you ever gone through a particularly rough day and the smallest, unexpected thing made you smile and feel joyful? If something as insignificant as a random cat rubbing his head on your leg can do that, don't you think that's enough reason to keep on doing it?"

27. Handicap

He had become a three-legged cat a few years earlier due to an accident and yet, he was rarely alone. Younger cats would approach him all the time looking for advice. They wanted to learn the best way of climbing a tree, how to hunt, or simply to listen to his stories. One day I asked him: "How did you become their mentor and have to deal with that handicap?"

Lying down on the ground, he blinked and stretched out. And then he said: "When they look at me, they don't see a three-legged cat. They see my survival skills and my resilience. So, I must thrive and teach them the best ways to survive. When someone believes in you so fiercely, the least you can do is believe in yourself at least as much as they do. And live by it."

28. Dark

He was still a cub, and yet he already was the most fearless cat I had ever known.

He was also particularly fond of dark places, so one day I asked him: "Aren't you afraid of the dark, not even a tiny bit?"

The tiny, brindle cat turned around to chase his own tail for a few seconds and then jumped towards me, before saying: "The only thing hiding in the dark is the other half of you, your fears and your self-imposed limits. When you dare to challenge them, how far can you go?"

Looking pretty proud of himself, he suddenly giggled and added: "But knowing you if you decide to hang out in the dark… please don't come barefoot."

29. Storm

We both found shelter at the entrance of the same building, while ahead of us the massive storm ripped the night with lightning and thunder. Watching the stripped cat standing next to me, I wondered why he wasn't panicking, and at the same time I felt glad he wasn't. But the moment I tried to reach for him, his ears became straight and he saw something I didn't. The next second he was gone, leaving me worried regarding his safety for a few seconds until I saw him again, walking towards me while carrying something. I could only figure out it was a kitten when he got closer, and I took off my coat to cover them both as soon as he made it to the building's entrance. Then I told him: "I thought you were gone for good, most cats would have lost it!"

He took a glance at me and shook his entire body before saying: "I suppose sometimes you only get to know your true nature during a storm."

30. Raindrops

Watching the young cat lying over the lap of his newly found human, I got closer to his ears and whispered: "How do we know we found the right person?"

While purring, his eyes half closed and a smile upon his tiny muzzle, he answered: "The right people always smell like the sunlight, and their touch feels like raindrops. Didn't you know love is made of sunlight and raindrops?"

31. Path

There's really nothing you can say to someone who, no matter how tough the path may turn out to be, refuses to give up on walking it on his own terms. We are talking about someone who is not afraid of looking foolish for choosing things that makes sense to his heart, someone who doesn't care how life can be hard as long as he gets to be where he wants. He doesn't care what everybody else thinks about him as long as his heart is at peace. One day I asked him: "Why do you always choose the hardest road?"

He lifted his tail and narrowed his eyes, and said: "Why do you assume I see any other way?"

32. Balance

He walked along the wooden fence in perfect balance, his paws touching each wooden board as if they were made of cotton clouds. I could actually feel the self-confidence overflowing from his yellow eyes, so I approached the fence a little farther ahead and waited for him: "Why hanging out so much on top of fences?"

He slowed the pace but didn't stop. He said, passing me by: "Life is pretty similar to walking on top of fences, you know? If you wish to keep your balance, you need to keep moving."

33. Be

He was the youngest of three cats belonging to the same family. He was used to being compared to the others all the time: "Put your eyes on Surya, he doesn't ruin any furniture!", "you could be gentler, Mia never scratches us!", or even "Mia doesn't climb over the table!" And yet, he reacted the same way every time, running away around the house as if it was his personal playground. One day I decided to ask him: "Aren't you tired of being compared to the others?"

He chased a fur ball towards me and grabbed one of my shoes with his tiny paws. Then he looked me straight in the eyes and said: "It's their job to compare me with them, not mine. I decided to just be who I am and let others decide who I should be."

34. Worth

I caught myself wondering how so many of us ended up choosing the wrong people to share our lives with, and I noticed the calico was staring at me as if he was guessing my thoughts. So, I asked him: "Why do you think that is?"

He lifted his head and yawned, before saying: "It isn't just people… sometimes we forget how special we are, and that makes us feel vulnerable and somewhat unworthy. When that happens, we end up picking the kind of love we think we deserve. Even if that's not true."

35. Happy Place

Every time life becomes too overwhelming, I enjoy getting out of the house and head towards an old tree standing tall nearby. Just by sitting underneath its branches I always felt relaxed, and it always helped me to breathe better. It was one of those days, while relaxing under the tree, I spotted the white cat for the first time. He was on top of the tree, watching me silently. Suddenly he got up, stretched out and sharpened his claws on a tree branch, before saying: "Isn't it amazing the way some places make us feel safe and at ease? Those are our happy places and they carry a tremendous power, pushing away everything that might be intoxicating us. Places like this are able to bring back to us life's true colors."

He stretched out again, and went back lying down on top of the branch. Then, he added: "Everyone should find a happy place."

36. Crowd

As a cat, he wouldn't allow anyone else to make decisions over his steps but himself. He spent most of his time alone and didn't seem to care. Actually, there was always an overflowing joy in the way he would climb over random rooftops just to catch the first sunrays in the morning, or the way he stretched out by the garden in the sunny afternoons. One day I asked him: "Isn't that little world of yours too lonely sometimes?"

The big Siamese stretched out for a second, his fur bristling for a moment while he extended his slim and yet elegant body. With his eyes closed he smelled the air for a second, before opening them to face me. He said: "What about you? Isn't it tiring to live in a world where the value of your steps is determined by an entire crowd?"

37. High view

The huge black cat could usually be found hanging out in one out of two places: he was either running around the house, chasing invisible enemies, or standing on top of some random piece of furniture. This time, I found him standing on top of a tall chair, watching his surroundings. I shrugged and asked him: "Are you watching over your kingdom from up there?"

He turned around to face me but kept leaning on the chair with his bulky tail waving behind him. He said: "Life is like this house, a mysterious maze full of decisions to make and doors we may or may not decide to open wide. Don't you agree that inside every maze as in life, sometimes a higher view can make a huge difference?"

38. Silence.

"**H**ave you ever wondered why cats move so silently?", the orange cat asked me one day, coming out of nowhere.

I shrugged and answered, my heart still racing: "To succeed on ambushes and avoid unexpected danger?"

He leaned his head against my leg and dropped his furry body towards the ground, looking amused: "Good call, but that's not the answer I'm looking for."

I shrugged again, bent down and cuddled his head behind his ears. A few seconds later, he added: "The most important decisions of your life will always leave a trail others may follow. But your success will always rely on how silent your steps come to be."

39. Friendship

Every time I laid down feeling sorry for myself, the tuxedo cat would show up coming out of nowhere and scratch my arm or my leg with his sharp claws. If it wasn't already bad enough to feel trapped in my own life, I also had to deal with the scratches. One day, after a particularly painful scratch, I yelled at him: "What's wrong with you? That hurts!"

He looked me straight in the eye and said: "Who's your best friend? The one allowing you to feel sorry for yourself for things you cannot change, or the one delivering you wake up calls and changing the focus of your thoughts?"

40. Love

Lying down in my arms with his eyes half-closed while I rubbed his tiny, furry head, the young cat resembled a working engine. Smiling, I asked him: "Why do cats purr?"

He opened his eyes a bit and stretched out, right before adjusting his body to my arms again. He yawned and said, before closing his eyes again: "Is there a better way to say I love you?"

41. Aquarium

I had seen him before, squeezing into some weird places like inside drawers, under rugs and even on top of open doors. But this time the gray cat was lying down inside an empty aquarium. He did nothing without a purpose, so I approached him and noticed he couldn't possibly be comfortable in there. As soon as I got near the aquarium, he lifted his head to stand above the glass and said: "We can always adapt to different circumstances, but just because you can fit inside an empty aquarium that doesn't mean you belong in there."

42. Be

I can't keep myself from wondering, maybe the deity has created the cat so that we could understand that the most powerful kind of love is the one overflowing from our ability to remain true to ourselves. A cat shares himself with the world, not what the world demands him to be.

43. Survival

O ne day a fox told an old cat: "Teach me the best ways of survival."

Afraid of being attacked, the old cat agreed. For the few weeks ahead, he taught the fox the best ways of hunting, fishing and even how to ambush her prey. Finally, when she thought she had learned enough, she approached the old cat and said: "You taught me well and now I'm ready. But I'm also starving, and you'll become my next prey."

In a second, the old cat jumped high in the air and climbed the nearest tree. The fox didn't know how to climb trees, so she remained in the ground and yelled: "You never taught me how to climb trees!"

Standing safe on top of a high branch, the old cat said: "You see when I first met you, life had already taught me how to survive. Do you want a final piece of advice?"

The fox frowned and agreed, so the old cat added: "Wherever life takes you, never dig a hole deeper than the range of your legs. Just in case you need to jump."

44. Complements

I sat next to him by the doorstep. With my back leaning against the closed door, it suddenly came to me how different we were, me and the gray cat standing beside me. And yet, we were very good friends. I asked him: "Isn't it odd, we becoming friends being so different from one another?"

He stood silent for a few seconds, which made me think he was probably ignoring me, but finally he said: "Only as odd as the fact that you need both a locker and a key to open a locked door. They're so different and yet, they complement each other so well."

45. Wounds.

He was a young cat, as curious as any cat can be. One day he approached an older cat and noticed there were scars all over his muzzle, so he asked him: "How did you manage to survive in a world that gave you so many scars?"

The older cat blinked and looked the younger cat straight in the eye. He said: "If you're willing to survive and explore the world, there are important decisions to be made. One day you'll feel the need to ask yourself: am I going to be led by my spirit, or by my wounds instead?"

46. Ugly

"**M**um, am I ugly?"

The black mother cat raised her eyebrows and asked the little black cat: "Why would you ever think that?"

The younger black cat sighed, and said: "They say I'm ugly because I'm black!"

The mother cat took a deep breath: "What color is the night sky?"

"Black…"

She smiled, and continued: "What color am I?"

The little black cat frowned: "Black…"

She nodded: "And have you ever seen me regret it?"

"No…"

His mother went serious for a second and said: "You must always feel proud of who you are. Ugly is not a color, it's a shameful word used by those not yet aware of how to listen to their own hearts."

47. Restless

The little cat was feeling restless and he wasn't quite sure why. He reached for his mother and began grabbing her waving tail. A few moments later, she said to him: "Are you hungry?"

The little cub frowned, her mother's tail waving in between his paws. He answered: "No."

The mother cat stood up, releasing her tail from its enclosure, and smiled. She replied: "There are two types of hunger: the one where you need to eat so your body remains healthy, and the one where you need to be happy so both your heart and your soul can remain healthy."

The little cat was confused: "What do you mean?"

The mother cat smiled, narrowing her eyes, and licked her son's forehead with her rough tongue. She said: "When you feel restless, it means your heart and soul are restless. And when that happens you need to feed them with your own happiness, that peaceful feeling showing up when you're doing everything you can to achieve your greatest potential as a living being."

48. Excuses

I rubbed the striped cat's chin while he stretched his claws and purred with his eyes closed. Suddenly I asked him: "Why are most of you cats so confident in your life decisions, and most humans remain so insecure when facing a difficult decision?"

He kept his eyes closed and rubbed his muzzle on my arm, his tail waving as in "give me a second to think about it". A few moments later he said: "I guess that happens because the day each of you decide to step into your own inner power, there will be no more excuses. No more turning back."

49. Hurry

I was in a hurry as usual, trying to get all my chores done and while I was into it, my cat chased me all around the house. Finally, when I managed to get everything done, I laid down in the couch and took a deep breath. A few seconds later I felt a bite on my arm and realized the cat had bit me, so I yelled: "Hey, what was that all about?"

He jumped over the couch and stared at me, looking confused. He said: "When you first adopted me I took an oath, I swore to protect you from any harm within my reach. When I saw you running around the house I thought something was chasing you, but there was nothing there! So, I figured you were being chased by your own hurry! The closest thing I could find was your arm, so I went for it!"

50. Fur

No matter what I did to prevent it, I was never able to leave the house without loads of white and orange fur all over my clothes. One day I went straight to the source and asked: "Will I ever be able to leave the house without taking a piece of you with me?"

The orange cat looked me straight in the eye and smiled. He said: "Why would you wish to do that? Every time you leave the house I miss you so much, and all I have left of you are your clothes! They smell just like you and that helps me not missing you so much. What's wrong with you carrying some of my fur around and do the same?"

51. Grounding

Every once in a while, I caught the huge tabby lying down on the floor, and I couldn't figure out why. One day I asked him: "You have your own bed, our bed, the couch and every other piece of furniture around the house available each time you wish to take a nap. Why lying on the floor?"

He lifted his head, blinking, and stretched his body along the wooden floor. After yawning, he answered: "My beloved human, Earth is like a mother to us. Every time our bodies become heavy by clearing out our families and surroundings from negative energies, we feel the need to lay down in her lap to recharge, delivering her the heaviness we previously collected from the world."

I frowned in disbelief, so he added: "Why do you think you find it so relaxing every time I start to purr while standing on your lap? Who do you think deals with the monsters I find under your bed?"

52. Perseverance

Every day when meals were served to the stray cat colony by the beach, a chubby cat would get there first and feast on the starving stray's food. One day, coming out of nowhere, a huge black cat joined the race. Even coming from far behind he took advantage of an unexpected sea wave, which made the chubby cat hesitate and lose the race towards the food. The black cat got there first and kept the house cat away. Later on, he told me: "You see, being successful has nothing to do with speed. It's all about perseverance. All you need to do is keep going as if there was no such thing as failure and seize the opportunity when it presents itself to you."

53. Fight

The majestic tuxedo cat was the most peaceful cat I had ever known, and yet that day I saw him get into a fight. A foreign, angry dog coming out of nowhere ran directly towards him and the usually calm cat turned into a wild panther right before my eyes in a matter of seconds. Finding himself cornered, he had no choice but to fight for his life, and so he did. And he won. As soon as I could I ran towards him, reaching him right after he chased the humiliated dog away. Still breathing heavily, he said to me: "You should never start a fight, but if you find yourself pushed into one, win."

54. Homeless

One day I approached a homeless man with a cat and after sharing some food with them both, I quietly asked the cat: "Why did you choose this man? It must be hard sharing a life in the streets!"

The tabby looked me in the eye for a second, as if deciding I was worthy of his story. A few moments later, he whispered: "Home is not a place. Don't get me wrong, it gets tough sometimes when it rains, and colder nights are hard to deal with. But for me, home is caring. He saved my life when no one else would, and we keep each other warm ever since. The easiest thing to do is to stand by someone when everything's fine. The true challenge is to stand by when everything goes wrong, and the ones who do it are the best ones: they love you for who you are, no matter how hard the path may become."

55. Hugs

Most cats I had crossed paths with in the past didn't like being hugged, so one day I had to ask the striped cat: "Why aren't most cats fond of hugs?"

My furry friend gave it a thought for a few seconds and said: "It all comes down to the kind of hug you're referring to, I guess. You see, dogs for instance, they teach humans how to hug with an open chest. Cats, on their turn, teach them how to hug with an open mind."

56. Noise

I took a deep breath and patiently cleaned up the remains of my tulip vase from all over the kitchen floor, while the huge white cat sat on the kitchen table, watching. Finally, I sighed and asked him: "Why did you do that? Was it a feng shui thing?"

He watched me finish the clean up and said: "Cats are silent most of the time, and after a while your fears and monsters under the bed convince themselves you're not protected anymore. But they're wrong, and we need to make some noise every once in a while, so that they become fully aware we still have your back."

57. Wild

He was as wild as a feral cat can be, but I was determined to earn his trust. Soon enough I realized it wasn't all about his mistrust towards human beings, he was also too proud to agree on being tamed. So, I gave up on turning him into a house pet but didn't give up on establishing a connection with him. I decided to try a different approach and started ignoring him instead. A few days later he silently approached me, so I said: "Thank you."

For no longer than a second, I could swear I saw him smile. He said: "It didn't take you that long to understand, I can respect you for that."

I caught myself smiling, and whispered back: "It was never about taming you, right?"

His bristled fur softened a bit, and he added: "No, it wasn't. If you wish to earn the trust of a wild animal, you must find the wild nature inside yourself. Only then you'll truly understand what it means to remain free. That's what this was all about."

58. Stars

He came out of the bushes and walked right towards me as if we were old friends, and yet I had never seen the immense tabby before. Besides, it was dark all around us and it felt like I also had darkness all over my heart that night. I figured he would leave as soon as he realized I had no food to share with him, but he didn't. He stopped a few inches away and just stood there, watching me. A few moments later he turned around, headed towards the bushes and I thought I wouldn't get to see him again. And yet, as soon as he reached for the bushes he didn't just walk through, he jumped over the bushes instead. Next thing I know, an entire crowd of fireflies took over the night all around us, leaving me speechless. It was the most beautiful scene I had ever seen in my life and from the distance, I heard the tabby cat say before walking away for good: "When you're under a dark, night sky, you mustn't just wait for the stars to rise and lighten up your view. Sometimes you need to lighten it up yourself."

59. Thunderstorm

I had never seen a cat being at ease during a thunderstorm, and yet the striped cat seemed to enjoy watching it through the living room window every time. His fur would always become a little bristled, but not even once had I ever seen him run away from any thunder or lightening clearing up the sky. One day I joined him and decided to ask: "Why aren't you afraid of thunderstorms like any other cat?"

He glanced at me and a new lightening was suddenly mirrored in his eyes. He answered: "You see, one day I realized I can't control the storm, or prevent it from happening. But the way I react to it, that's totally up to me."

60. Habits

He was a former stray cat, now spending most of his days lying down on the couch which belonged to his new family. He used to be hard tempered, so one day I asked him: "Getting used to your new life is making you softer, hum?"

He glanced at me with his stunning emerald eyes and said, after stretching out: "Habits are funny things, you know? When you're out there surviving on your own, a good habit can save your life. After becoming an indoor cat, though, you can switch off your survival mode. It is a really cool thing about habits: some of them can save your life, and others allow you to fully enjoy it."

61. Memories

I didn't know what sort of memories the orange cat carried from the years spent in the streets, therefore I wasn't yet sure of the best way to communicate with him. So, I handled a broom near him and I saw fear in his eyes; I picked a small rock from the ground and he ran away for cover. But then I made him smell lavender and he closed his eyes purring, I lit the fire pit and he stood there, relaxed, enjoying the tender heat coming out of the flames. And suddenly it came to me: memories aren't made of what was seen, they emerge from what was felt. You don't remember something because of the way it looked like, you remember it because of the way it made you feel.

He turned his head around to look at me, the flames from the fire pit still dancing in his eyes. He said: "That's it. Now you know."

62. Full Moon

Feeling nostalgic, I decided to head outside and appreciate the full moon for a while. It didn't take long for the striped cat to show up and join me, so I decided to ask him: "Why can't we be like the full moon and feel fulfilled and shiny all the time?"

He jumped over the fence and stood right next to my head, side by side with the full moon in the sky. He said: "Don't you see? The moon doesn't need to be always full to be whole."

63. Inner claws

"Grab it with your inner claws", he told me one day, "a thousand times, grab it with your inner claws!"

I frowned. What was the black cat talking about? He sighed and approached me, lifting his paw to reach me, and added: "There's nothing happening outside of you, that didn't already happen inside. So, when you have a big goal, you need to grab it with your inner claws first, so when the time comes to fight for it outside in the world, your goal has already proven itself to you."

I was confused, so I asked: "What's the big difference between inner claws and regular claws?"

He glanced at me with his eyes glowing and said: "Your regular claws are meant to help you thrive in the outside world, and your inner claws are meant to help you thrive within yourself."

64. Trust

No matter what I did, the tabby cat would always keep her distance. She did talk to me every once in a while, but always from a distance. One day I asked her: "Would it be that bad if you decided to trust me for a change?"

She glanced at me with her eyes sparkling, the wind swirling all around her on top of the wooden wall and said: "Don't you get it? I only speak to whom I trust. You're the one dealing with trusting issues if you believe I don't trust you just because I won't let you touch me."

I frowned, so she added: "you need to accept me for who I am, and acknowledge the kind of bond we share."

I took a deep breath and smiled, feeling closer to her than ever. She hadn't moved an inch, her eyes sparkling when she spoke once more: "you see, the biggest distance stands between what is and what we think should be."

65. Happiness

Being a former stray cat, he had been through a lot while roaming the streets before he was adopted by a loving family. Yet these days he was most likely to be found in the garden, hanging out among the flowers. Watching him narrow his eyes while smelling a daisy, I felt like asking: "You've been through a lot in your youth, how come your favorite thing is being out here smelling the flowers? Is it really that simple?"

The elder cat gently rubbed his forehead against the daisy and glanced at me. Then he took a deep breath and said: "Looking back may be a tough call when you've had a rough start in life. But despite what you've been through, being happy will always be a choice, not a consequence."

66. Sunset

I noticed the gray cat outside enjoying the sunset and decided to join him. A few moments later I sighed and he glanced at me, so I rubbed his head and said: "I'm sorry, I'm a worrier and I was just thinking the sun is already down in the horizon and there's still so much to do."

He got up, stretched up and said, while facing the reddish sun: "You can't just watch the sunset without hearing what it has to say. Same with pretty much everything around you."

I frowned, feeling confused, so he added: "what is the sunset telling you?"

I shrugged, which made him wave his tail and answer his own question: "you need to follow the sunset's lead… and fulfill your destiny without rushing it."

67. Scars

The overflowing confidence coming out of her eyes made me feel inspired every time, and yet it was common knowledge the calico had been to a few scary places during her lifetime so far. One day I asked her: "Every inch of your body exhales strength and majesty and yet I know you've been through some hardships in the past. How come you're not afraid of life?"

She glanced at me and blinked while taking a deep breath, and the life passion I've seen inside her eyes stunned me once again. Noticing it, she narrowed her eyes in a smile and said: "My scars are my best friends, and I wear them with pride. They remind me I'm stronger than misfortune and they also map the places I don't want to go back to. You see, the funny thing about life is you don't really need to know where you're headed... you just need to figure out where you're not."

68. Joy

The black cat didn't care what everyone else was saying or doing, he chose to live his life as if the entire world was his playground instead. One day, noticing I was watching him chase a loose feather, he blinked at me. So, I asked him: "Don't you ever get sad or frustrated? Have you never come across a door your joy wasn't able to open wide?"

He watched as the feather gently landed on the ground for a second and then he walked towards me, sitting down only a few inches away. Staring at me, he finally said: "Feeling joyful won't open every door for you. But will help you figure out every meaningful door can only be opened from within."

69. Compassion

He was a stray cat no one paid attention to, but that day he spotted a tiny kitty crying for help in the middle of a busy road, lying helpless among the traffic. Standing on the sidewalk there was a girl crying out loud, afraid of crossing the road to go pick him up. Not a single driver stopped, neither did anyone passing by. The stray closed his eyes for a second and took a deep breath, before facing the ongoing cars at his own risk and gave it a try on saving the kitten. He grabbed the little one by the neck while trying not to be ran over and brought him back to the little girl, dropping him by her feet. She quickly picked him up, tears still dropping down from her cheeks, and walked away. When the stray got closer, I asked him: "Why did you risk your life? You don't mean anything to them."

He bended his head and looked me deeply in the eyes, before saying: "I didn't do it for them, but for the sake of the little one. You see, they don't have to like you. You just need to care."

70. Speech

I looked up on the black cat due to his ability to communicate with other beings, regardless of them being cats or belonging to any other species. One day I told him: "I admire the way you make yourself clear to everyone and not just other cats. Sometimes I think maybe humans talk too much and feel too little."

He bended his head and stared at me, as if measuring my words. Finally, he smiled and said: "One day humans will realize most of the time they speak to be seen, not to be heard."

I raised my eyebrow, feeling confused. He narrowed his eyes and added: "If you wish to be seen, use words. If you wish to be heard, rely on your silent actions."

71. Wisdom

One day I asked a black cat passing me by: "What's the secret to a happy life?"

He ceased his steps but didn't look back, glancing at the horizon ahead. A few moments later, he said: "Never allow your eyes to speak to you so loud, that you're not able to listen to your heart whisper anymore."

His words caught me off guard, so I told him: "Wise words from a black cat!"

This time he turned his head around to face me and added: "Everything your eyes could see was a random black cat, and yet your heart knew I was worth reaching for."

72. Love

The little girl was cuddling her black cat and it was the sweetest thing to watch, I was able to feel the bond between them and how much they loved each other. After a while I asked her: "What's your favorite color in a cat?"

She smiled and answered me back right away: "Felix's color!"

I smiled: "So your favorite color for a cat is black?"

She frowned: "No! It's Felix's color!"

When she left the room for a while, the black cat came to me and rubbed his head on my leg, before saying: "Don't you get it? Her favorite color for a cat is love!"

73. Worries

I was feeling so sad that day, and as lonely as anyone can feel sometimes. And yet the tuxedo cat stretched his paw and reached for my hand. I said: "I'm sorry, I'm not feeling very lovable right now."

He looked me straight in the eyes and answered: "You already know I love you, that's not what I'm saying. I'm saying don't worry, I've got you."

74. Abyss

Life can be harsh sometimes. And every once in a while, we may even end up with a few scars to show for it. And yet a few of those scars will remain unnoticed, hidden from the sight and only felt in the heart. The orange tabby had a torn ear and yet he didn't seem to care, his eyes speaking of overcome challenges, and he was undoubtedly in love with life. One day I asked him: "How do you deal with those scars of yours?"

He glanced at me and the overflowing wisdom coming from his eyes stunned me. He said: "Scars are either to be seen or felt. Most of the time they are both. So, you need to deal with the way you feel about them first of all. You see, it all comes down to realizing each scar of yours is shaped like a strong paw... and you're supposed to use those paws to jump over the abyss."

75. Clouds

" **A**ren't you a bit too small to reach for the sky?", I asked the gray cat one day, noticing him watching the clouds as if traveling among them.

He dropped his glance back down to Earth and blinked, shaking his head. Then he took a deep breath and said: "reaching for the sky has nothing to do with heights."

I frowned: "what do you mean?"

He smiled, narrowing his eyes and rubbing his head against my knee. He added: "It's not about getting up there, humans have planes for that. It's about finding the sky within ourselves and be free."

76. Self-confidence

"I wish I was as self-confident as you are", I told the black cat one day.

He bowed his head and frowned, his yellow eyes wide open in disbelief: "you got this all wrong."

It was my turn to frown, what did he mean? He noticed my confusion and stood up, stretched his body and yawned. Then he came closer to me and whispered: "Don't you see? It's not about who you are, it all comes down to who you think you're not."

77. Vampires

I had left the night before to meet some friends and came back home feeling exhausted. Next morning, I was still feeling somewhat numb so I fed the cat and went straight to the couch to lay down for a while. A few moments later I realized my cat had followed me, so I asked: "why aren't you eating your breakfast?"

He bent his head and faced me, his long tail waving behind him. He said: "what do you know about vampires?"

I frowned: "do you mean the bats?"

He shook his head and a bunch of fur whirled in the air all around him: "No. Human vampires, and not the ones from movies."

I raised my eyebrows, so he added: "Human vampires don't suck blood, they suck energy by demanding your attention. Look at you, you're drained... I bet at least one of your friends is a vampire."

78. Prejudice

Sadly, many people nowadays still consider black cats are evil or uninteresting due to their coat's color. So, when I crossed paths with him that day, I asked him: "Why do you think some people still hold prejudice against black cats?"

He stood silent for a few seconds, his tail waving. Finally, he said: "does it matter?"

I blushed, so he rubbed his head on my leg and added: "Some of your ancestors decided we were evil once, so nowadays some of you still either hate or fear us."

I frowned: "And that doesn't bother you?"

He smiled and started to walk away, and I could hear him say from the distance: "Why should I? My ancestors, on their turn, happened to be wild panthers."

79. Regrets

I watched him while he entered the room, the elegance overflowing his shiny, white coat. I asked him: "Do you have any regrets in life?"

He sat down next to the white wall and glanced at me: "We all regret something every once in a while. It's not about if we do, but rather on how well you cope with them. Look behind me, can't you see? Even a white cat owns a dark shadow."

80. Unconditionally

I was sitting outside watching the tuxedo cat chase a butterfly among the flowers. Suddenly the butterfly decided she had enough and flew away, so he ran towards me and rubbed his head on my leg. I said: "People often say animals love unconditionally, is that right?"

He jumped over my lap and bowed his head, then licked his tiny paw and rubbed it all over his muzzle for a few seconds. Finally, he said: "That unconditional love of yours… what does it mean?"

I frowned while rubbing his head and said: "It means loving without restrictions, without asking for anything in return."

He frowned: "Even if you're loving someone not right for you?"

I didn't know what to say, so he added: "You see, we do love unconditionally and that's fine. But unconditional unhappiness is not."

81. Choices

The tiny cat was improving his climbing skills every day, but not without getting bruised every now and then. One day, after watching him land on his back after a failed attempt on jumping over a high chair, I said: "You should be more careful, or you'll end up hurting yourself."

He stepped back, ready to try again, and said without even glancing at me: "The way I see it, we have two choices in life: either we get hurt by staying where we are, or we get hurt while chasing our limits and challenging ourselves."

82. Humbleness

The night before, a huge storm had taken down a huge tree nearby, so the next morning the orange cat accompanied me while checking out the damage. As we got closer, we were able to witness the immense tree roots coming out of the ground as if grabbed and pulled off by a giant, a sad thing to watch. Suddenly he jumped over the tree trunk and said: "What does this tell you about life?"

I frowned, still overwhelmed by the sight of that once magnificent tree now lying down on the ground. As I stood silent, he finally said: "You see, in life, it doesn't really matter how strong you are, if you're not willing to bend over every once in a while. Staying humble may prevent you from becoming a victim of you own pride."

83. Elder

Everyone in the neighborhood knew the old black cat. Even his kind respected him and came to him often, asking for help or advice. One day, a foreigner came by and approached the elder: "We are all survivors, what makes you special among the rest of us?"

Suddenly a younger cat walked towards them, limping, and asked the old cat for help. The foreigner quickly said: "It's probably broken, there's nothing we can do for him."

The elder gently checked the younger cat's paw pad and spotted a thorn, which he immediately pulled out with his teeth.

"Any of us could have done that!", the foreigner said.

The younger cat frowned and replied: "You're right, but only the elder knew where to look."

84. Change

The black, old cat was lying down next to his filled-up food bowl, his eyes half-closed, watching me vent. Suddenly he yawned and said: "Why are you struggling?"

I sighed and replied: "I'm trying to figure out how to become a better person."

He bent his head and frowned: "No wonder you're so angry at yourself, you're trying to add water to an already full cup!"

I was confused: "What do you mean?"

The old cat stretched out and pointed out his food bowl: "Look at it, it's full because I'm not hungry yet. If I tried to eat all that food now, I would get sick. Likewise, if you're trying to become a better person, you'll have to empty yourself from the old you, first."

85. Action

"I'm always told I must listen to my heart", I told the tabby one day, "but sometimes it doesn't change anything."

She glanced at me with her emerald eyes for a second, and gently placed her paw over my leg: "listening to your heart may change the way you feel and open the path before your eyes, but if you wish to see real changes that's not enough."

I frowned: "what do you mean?"

She licked her paw and rubbed her muzzle for a second, then she replied: "Sometimes listening won't be enough, and you'll need to talk yourself into acting upon it as well."

86. Decisions

The black cat stretched out his paw and saved the little snake from drowning. A few moments later the snake crawled away and I approached him: "You saved that snake, any chance it was poisonous?"

He glanced at me and yawned, stretching out his entire body: "Does it matter?"

I frowned: "What if she bites anyone else, didn't you think of that? If she does, it will be your fault!"

He turned around to face me: "I saved a life, that's on me. I'm not responsible for anyone else's decisions."

87. Rock

While taking a walk outside, I stumbled on a loose rock and fell to the ground. My knees started to ache and I stood down, grunting. In a matter of seconds, the striped cat came out of the bushes and walked right towards me: "Are you ok?"

I glanced at him, feeling grumpy: "Look at me, I'm hurt! Do I look ok?"

He bent his head, his tail waving: "Do you know what's even worse than stumbling on a rock and getting hurt?"

I frowned, so he added: "getting attached to the rock."

88. Darkness

Sometimes we find ourselves in a dark place, overwhelmed by our own thoughts. Watching me burn inside, the grey cat approached me and rubbed his body against my leg. He yawned and said: "You see, you can get rid of your inner darkness as much as the sun can get rid of shadows. It's not about overcoming darkness, it's about learning to love yourself despite its existence.

89. Nomad

The black cat was a nomad. One day he spotted a kitten being bullied and he helped him escape. Next thing they were both leaving the village. I approached them and asked the kitten: "What did he tell you? Why are you leaving with him?"

The younger cat took a deep breath and whispered: "he told me that sometimes, having no reason to stay is a good reason to go."

The End

Manufactured by Amazon.ca
Bolton, ON

10216770R10059